ENCYCLOPEDIA of PRESIDENTS

Forty-First President of the United States

By Zachary Kent

Consultant: Charles Abele, Ph.D.
Social Studies Instructor
Chicago Public School System

CHILDRENS PRESS®
CHICAGO

President Bush poses with his family in the White House, January 21, 1989.

Library of Congress Cataloging-in-Publication Data

Kent, Zachary.
George Bush / by Zachary Kent.
p. cm. — (Encyclopedia of presidents)
Includes index.
Summary: A biography emphasizing the political career of the forty-first president.
ISBN 0-516-01374-2
1. Bush, George, 1924- —Juvenile literature.
2. Presidents—United States—Biography—Juvenile literature. 3. United States—Politics and government—1981-1989—Juvenile literature. 4. Presidents—United States—Election—1988—Juvenile literature.
5. Presidents—United States—Election—1980—Juvenile literature. [1. Bush, George, 1924-
2. Presidents.] I. Title. II. Series.
E882.K46 1989
973.928'092—dc20 89-33744
[B] CIP
[92] AC

Picture Acknowledgments

AP/Wide World Photos, Inc.—David Valdez, 4; 5, 14, 17, 18, 21, 26, 33, 38, 42, 45, 49, 50, 62, 65, 66, 71, 76, 77, 78, 88, 89

Midland Desk & Derrick Collection, The Petroleum Museum, Midland, Texas—29

Official U.S. Navy Photograph—8, 24

Official White House Photograph—David Valdez, 2, 82, 85, 86; 6, 11, 12, 25, 31, 32, 39, 40, 46, 48, 54

UPI/Bettmann Newsphotos—34, 36, 37, 51, 53 (2 photos), 58, 61, 69, 70, 72, 75, 80, 81, 87

Cover design and illustration by Steven Gaston Dobson

Printed in the United States of America.
1 2 3 4 5 6 7 8 9 10 R 98 97 96 95 94 93 92 91 90 89

George Bush, with Dan Quayle in the background, accepts his nomination.

Table of Contents

LIFE JACKET

Chapter 1

"I Was Alive and Had a Chance"

Across the deck of the light aircraft carrier USS *San Jacinto*, dozens of navy pilots scrambled for action. For three years in the Pacific Ocean the United States had been locked in bloody war against Japan. On that morning of September 2, 1944, the men of the VT-51 torpedo squadron prepared to attack the Japanese island of Chi Chi Jima, 500 miles south of Tokyo.

Lieutenant Junior Grade George Bush climbed aboard a single-engine TBM Avenger bomber with the nickname "Barbara" painted on its side. The tall, lanky twenty-year-old pilot was a veteran of many missions. He fully understood the dangers of this Chi Chi Jima raid. "We took off on schedule. . . , " he later remembered. "After I was harnessed in, my plane was hooked onto the catapult. I ran it up full-throttle, gave the catapult officer my arm-across-the-chest signal, and was launched skyward."

Opposite page: Navy pilot Bush in the cockpit of his bomber

A VT-51 TBM Avenger bomber launched from the USS *San Jacinto*

Springing by catapult off the carrier deck, Bush spent the next hour raising his plane to an altitude of 12,000 feet. The two men in his crew that day, tail gunner Jack Delaney and turret gunner William G. White, joined Bush in scanning the sky for enemy activity. At last the raiding party, consisting of planes from several American carriers, neared the Chi Chi Jima coast.

"The flak was the heaviest I'd ever flown into," Bush afterwards exclaimed. "The Japanese were ready and waiting; their antiaircraft guns were set to nail us as we pushed into our dives. By the time the VT-51 was ready to go in, the sky was thick with angry black clouds of exploding antiaircraft fire."

Squadron leader Donald Melvin swooped in first. His bombs scored direct hits, blasting a Japanese radio tower. Steering his Avenger into a dive, Bush bravely followed. He strained to see the target area. Black splotches of flak popped all around his plane.

"Suddenly there was a jolt," Bush later declared, "as if a massive fist had crunched into the belly of the plane. Smoke poured into the cockpit, and I could see flames rippling across the crease of the wing, edging toward the fuel tanks."

Although his damaged plane might explode at any moment, Bush still headed for his target. He dropped his four 500-pound bombs before heading back out to sea.

"Once over water," he recalled, "I leveled off and told Delaney and White to bail out. . . . " Choking smoke swirled through the crippled plane as Bush jumped out. "The wind was playing tricks," remembered the young officer, "or more likely, I pulled the rip cord too soon. First my head, then my parachute canopy collided with the tail of the plane." As the plane sped past his falling figure, the tail gashed his forehead and tore through the silk of his parachute.

"I came down fast—because of the torn canopy," Bush exclaimed, "faster than I wanted." After hitting the water, he quickly slipped out of his parachute to keep from being dragged under. He searched the water around him, but saw no sign of Delaney and White. Sadly, Bush later learned that neither of his crewmen had survived. One went down with the crashing plane. The other bailed out, but his parachute failed to open.

While the air battle raged high above him, Bush bobbed in the water. Luckily his squadron buddies did their best to help him. "My seatback rubber raft was somewhere in the area," he recalled, "but if it hadn't been for Don Melvin swooping down, then up, to signal its location, I'd never have seen it, much less swum to it." Avenger pilot Doug West spotted a couple of Japanese boats from Chi Chi Jima cutting through the waves toward Bush. West and other squadron members strafed these enemy boats with machine-gun fire, forcing them to turn back. West also dropped a medical kit down to his injured friend.

"My head still ached," remembered Bush as he sat alone in his rubber raft. "Still I was alive and had a chance." Nervously he hoped an American ship would come to pick him up, realizing that "if nothing showed up that day, my luck might have run out." Through the next minutes Bush paddled furiously. "A half hour passed," he remembered. "An hour. An hour and a half. There was no sign of activity from the island, no Japanese headed my way. But nothing else was headed my way either."

Finally Bush spied a small black dot rising in the water just one hundred yards away. "The dot grew larger," he later declared. "First a periscope, then the conning tower, then the hull of a submarine emerged from the depths."

"My rescue ship was the USS *Finback*," Bush exclaimed. A *Finback* officer, Ensign Bill Edwards, even stood on the bridge of the sub's conning tower, filming the event with a small camera. "Welcome aboard!" called out a sailor, as he pulled Bush out of his raft. "Let's get below. The skipper wants to get the hell out of here."

Bush (standing, second from right) with his navy buddies

"On shaky legs I climbed down the conning tower into the hold of the *Finback*," recalled Bush with relief. "The hatches slammed shut, the horns sounded, and the sub's skipper gave the order, 'Take her down.' "

Bush never forgot his close call. "I'll always be grateful to the *Finback* crew," he stated years later. "They saved my life." For his courage during the Chi Chi Jima raid, the navy awarded Bush the Distinguished Flying Cross.

After a month aboard the *Finback*, he returned to flying combat. Through a total of fifty-eight missions the modest young officer showed his sense of duty again and again. Hardy patriotism, loyal comradeship, and a deep belief in public service had been the greatest lessons of George Bush's upbringing. After the war he continued to live by those ideals. Americans watched his steady rise through thirty years of politics. With trust and admiration, they elected him forty-first United States president in 1988.

Chapter 2

"Poppy" Bush

"I have led a privileged life," George Herbert Walker Bush has freely stated. Born in Milton, Massachusetts, on June 12, 1924, the infant traveled with his family when they moved to Greenwich, Connecticut, in 1925. In that wealthy suburban town young George grew up with three brothers and a sister.

"My father, Prescott Bush, Sr., was a successful businessman," he later recalled, "a partner in the investment banking firm of Brown Brothers, Harriman and Company." Every day Prescott Bush journeyed one hour south to his Wall Street office in New York City. Intelligent and hardworking, the handsome, six-foot-four-inch Bush naturally commanded the respect of his fellow workers and his children.

George's mother, Dorothy Walker Bush, was a lovely little brown-haired woman, always full of energy. "Mother was a first-rate athlete," her son remembered. "She wasn't big, but she was a match for anyone in tennis, golf, basketball, baseball—for that matter I don't recall a footrace Mother was ever in that she didn't come in first."

Opposite page: George as a toddler

George and his sister

George's parents came from well-to-do families, and Prescott Bush earned enough so that his children could live in comfort during the difficult years of America's Great Depression. The Bush home in Greenwich was a great "barn of a house." A live-in maid dusted the nine bedrooms. In the kitchen a full-time cook prepared the meals. When little George entered the private Greenwich Country Day School, a chauffeur drove him each day in the family car. In this carefree atmosphere the youngster spent many happy hours. "Life was easy in those days," his mother fondly remembered. "We had a lot of help. All the children had a lot of friends who were always swarming around the house."

George's parents, however, insisted their children learn high moral values and refused to let them become spoiled. "Dad taught us about duty and service," George later explained. "Mother taught us about dealing with life on a personal basis, relating to other people. . . . They were our biggest boosters, always there when we needed them. They believed in an old-fashioned way of bringing up a family—generous measures of both love and discipline."

Dorothy Bush disliked boastfulness in her children. Instead she encouraged them to be fair and generous. As an outgoing, friendly child, young George easily learned his mother's lessons. Every time he was given candy or cookies he would turn to the person next to him and say, "Here, have half." His constant willingness to share soon won him his family nickname, "Have Half." At school George's teachers graded him as a good student. In sports the youngster showed himself a natural athlete. With good nature, his brothers and sister openly admitted George was the star of the family. "They accepted from the start that George was going to be the best in whatever activity," declared his mother.

"We were a close, happy family," George remembered of his childhood, "and never closer or happier than when we crammed into the station wagon each summer—five kids, two dogs, with Mother driving—to visit Walker's Point in Kennebunkport, Maine." Dorothy Bush's father, George Herbert Walker, was a wealthy Saint Louis businessman. On eleven acres of craggy rocks, jutting out from the Maine coast, Grandfather Walker had built a summer home in 1901.

Into this sprawling, twenty-six-room "cottage" the Bush family cheerfully carried suitcases and boxes every summer. Delighted friends and relatives often filled every spare bedroom. Each day the Bush children splashed and swam in the water or whacked tennis balls at the local River Club. At night they gathered around the table to play backgammon or Scrabble. On weekends Prescott Bush arrived by train from work in New York City. For fun, he gathered family and friends for after-dinner songfests.

"For the younger members of the Bush family," remembered George, "Maine in the summer was the best of all possible adventures." The ocean off Walker's Point offered special wonders. "We'd spend long hours looking for starfish and sea urchins, while brown crabs scurried around our feet. . . . Then there was the adventure of climbing aboard my grandfather's lobster boat, *Tomboy*, to try our luck fishing. . . . It was Grandfather Walker who first taught us how to handle and dock a boat." George had been named in honor of his Grandfather George Herbert Walker, and everyone lovingly called the old man "Pop." In time, the family fondly took to calling young George "Little Pop," and soon the nickname "Poppy" stuck.

Upon graduating from the Greenwich Country Day School, "Poppy" Bush next entered private Phillips Academy in Andover, Massachusetts. Strolling about its lovely campus, he easily made friends with his new classmates. Teachers also complimented the young teenager's good manners and pleasantness. In the classroom, however, English instructor Hart Leavitt recalled that George "showed no imagination or originality."

George (left) with a friend at about the age of fourteen

Clearly Poppy preferred playing sports to studying. During his years in Andover he grew fast. Soon standing over six feet tall, he appeared rather gawky. Still, scooping ground balls off the grass as a first baseman on the baseball team, he proved himself a graceful athlete. Fast legwork and kicking ability made him a star of the soccer team. One Phillips Academy sports book noted: "Poppy Bush's play throughout the season ranked him as one of Andover's all-time soccer greats."

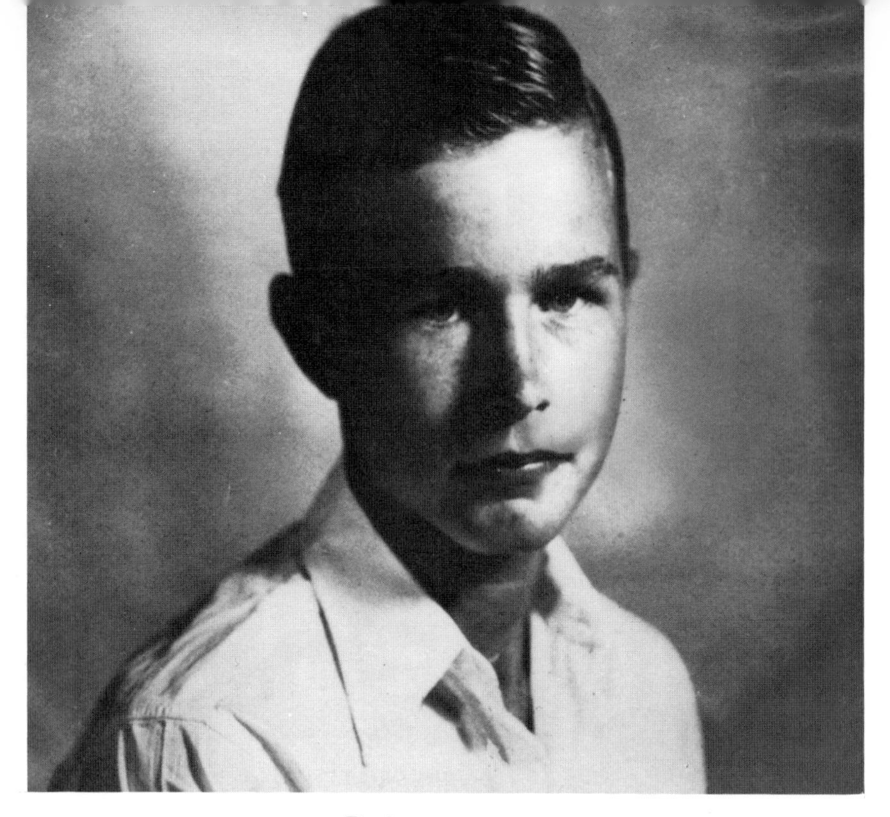

Bush as a teenager

Illness during a flu epidemic kept George sick at home for several months during his junior year. Returning to Andover with renewed energy, though, he became "president or captain of just about everything," recalled classmate Peter Welch. In his senior class poll, Bush ranked among the top four students in a number of categories: Best All-Round Fellow, Best Athlete, Most Respected, Most Popular, and Handsomest.

Sudden world events changed the course of George's life during his final year at Phillips Academy. On a Sunday morning in December, sirens wailed and sailors dove for cover as squads of Japanese planes bombed the U.S. naval base at Pearl Harbor, Hawaii. Outraged Americans demanded revenge for the sneak attack. Congress immediately declared war, thrusting the United States into active combat in World War II.

In the excitement of the moment, seventeen-year-old George Bush quickly vowed to do his patriotic duty. "When the Japanese bombed Pearl Harbor, December 7, 1941," he explained, "there wasn't any doubt which branch of the service I'd join. My thoughts immediately turned to naval aviation. College was coming up the following fall, but that would have to wait. The sooner I could enlist, the better."

Talk of the war filled the air. As he finished his school year, though, George still took time for fun. At Christmas time, he attended a prep-school dance in Greenwich. "The band was playing Glenn Miller tunes when I approached a friend from Rye, New York, Jack Wozencraft, to ask if he knew a girl across the dance floor, the one wearing the green-and-red holiday dress. He said she was Barbara Pierce, that she lived in Rye and went to school in South Carolina . . . he introduced us. . . . It was a storybook meeting."

While the band played, the two teenagers sat and talked, getting to know each other. Sixteen-year-old Barbara Pierce was the pretty daughter of the publisher of *McCall's* magazine. She was visiting home during her holiday school break from private Ashley Hall in Charleston, South Carolina. Barbara never forgot that Christmas dance, either. "George Bush was just the most beautiful-looking creature I ever laid my eyes on," she later revealed, ". . . the nicest person I'd ever met." "He was the first boy I ever kissed," she also admitted.

Shyly the young couple started dating. "I liked him and he liked me," she explained, "and that 'like' grew into an enormous love." "Barbara and I . . . progressed from simply being 'serious,' to meeting and spending time with each other's families," George remembered, "—a fairly important step for teenagers in those days."

As the war raged, however, George never forgot his desire to join the navy. In June 1942 he finally collected his graduation diploma from Phillips Academy. With his father's permission, he enlisted in the Naval Reserve almost immediately afterwards.

"On my eighteenth birthday," he declared, "I went to Boston and was sworn into the Navy as a Seaman Second Class. Not long thereafter, I was on a railway coach headed south for Navy preflight training in [Chapel Hill] North Carolina."

"I'd joined up to fly . . . ," Bush exclaimed. "I was gung ho to strap on the leather helmet and goggles the day I arrived at Chapel Hill. Because of the pilot shortage, the Navy had trimmed its aviator training course to ten months, but there weren't any shortcuts." First Bush studied the science of flying and the mechanics of planes in the classroom. Months later he jumped at the chance to fly trainer planes.

"In flight training at Corpus Christi [Texas] and along the East Coast," he recalled, "we were taught to gauge wind velocity and the height of waves." Finally, in the spring of 1943, he received his officer's commission. Having won his wings, Bush at the age of eighteen became the youngest pilot in the U.S. Navy.

Opposite page: Bush after he was commissioned in the navy

Of course, he still saw Barbara Pierce at every opportunity. That August she joined the Bush family at Kennebunkport. "Between boating and fishing excursions," revealed Bush, "we were secretly engaged," although, he added, "we knew that marriage was years away. . . . In the fall of 1943 I was assigned to VT-51, a torpedo squadron being readied for active duty in the Pacific."

The VT-51 squadron served aboard the light aircraft carrier USS *San Jacinto*, where Bush flew TBM Avenger torpedo bombers. "Like most TBM Avenger pilots," Bush explained, "I liked the teamwork and camaraderie that went with being part of a three-man crew." Through the next year, tail gunner Jack Delaney and turret gunner Leo Nadeau soared into combat with Bush again and again. "[We flew] missions over Wake Island, Palau, Guam, and Saipan," recounted Bush, "and survived a fair number of close calls, including a ditching operation when our plane sprang a leak. . . ." Altogether during the war Bush lost four planes because of malfunctions or battle damage. On each of his planes the young pilot painted the name of his fiancée, Barbara.

On September 2, 1944, near the Bonin Islands, Bush endured his most difficult experience as a navy flier. "It was the second day of concentrated air strikes . . . by our squadron . . . ," he recalled, and "the target for that day was a [Japanese] radio communications center on Chi Chi Jima, one of the three islands in the Bonin chain." That day gunnery officer William G. White got permission to take Leo Nadeau's place on Bush's plane. "Nobody had to remind us that the going would be rough," declared Bush.

Japanese antiaircraft fire pounded the sky with flak, as Bush's Avenger dove toward its target. A sudden, spine-shaking crack told the young pilot his plane was hit by gunfire. Still he dropped his bombs as scheduled before bailing out over the sea. With signaled help from a comrade flying above, Bush found his inflatable raft. "Where were Delaney and White?" the dazed flier wondered. Tragically, neither of his crewmen had survived the raid.

Through the next dangerous minutes Bush awaited rescue. "Alone in my raft, my squadron headed back to the carrier, I was slowly drifting toward Chi Chi Jima," he remembered. At last a submarine periscope poked up through the water. Surprised and grateful, Bush scrambled aboard the USS *Finback*.

For a month, he and three other rescued navy pilots remained aboard the *Finback* while it finished its combat patrol. "People talk about the risk of combat flying," Bush later declared, but "running on the surface, we were attacked by a Japanese Nell bomber. Below the surface, we were depth-charged: the sub would shudder . . . ."

At the end of the *Finback*'s hazardous patrol, Bush gladly stepped ashore again. For his "heroism and extraordinary achievement" over Chi Chi Jima, he earned the navy's Distinguished Flying Cross. The loss of his crewmen deeply saddened him, but he was ready to fly again. "I rejoined the *San Jacinto* and VT-51 exactly eight weeks after being shot down," he recalled, "in time to take part in strikes against enemy positions and shipping in the Philippines." Before the war's end, Bush won three combat air medals and was promoted to lieutenant.

The navy's Distinguished Flying Cross medal

"In December," he explained, "VT-51 was replaced by a new squadron, and after flying fifty-eight combat missions I was ordered home. No reunion could have been scripted more perfectly. I arrived Christmas Eve. There were tears, laughs, hugs, joy, the love and warmth of family in a holiday setting." Tightly holding one another, George and Barbara agreed not to postpone their marriage any longer. Barbara promptly dropped out of Smith College. Just two weeks later, on January 6, 1945, twenty-year-old George Bush and nineteen-year-old Barbara

George and Barbara Bush dancing at their wedding

Pierce exchanged loving wedding vows at the First Presbyterian Church in Rye, New York.

Lieutenant Bush's next military assignment took the young newlyweds to Oceana Naval Air Station, Virginia. He and other pilots prepared for the invasion of Japan. In August 1945, however, President Harry Truman ordered America's new atomic bombs dropped on the Japanese cities of Hiroshima and Nagasaki. Completely stunned by this nuclear destruction, Japan immediately surrendered. After four long years the war was finally over.

YALE

Chapter 3

Texas Oilman

"We were still young, life lay ahead of us, and the world was at peace. It was the best of times," Bush declared. In the fall of 1945 the young navy veteran and his wife moved to New Haven, Connecticut, where he entered Yale University. Fellow students who admired his cheerful personality invited Bush to join Yale's secret club, called Skull and Bones. They also elected him senior class president. Eager to finish his education, he studied hard as an economics major. Top grades earned him membership in the Phi Beta Kappa honorary fraternity.

"Technically my minor was sociology, but only technically," recalled Bush of his Yale years. "My real minors, as far as my attention span went, were soccer and baseball. Especially baseball." Bush practiced hours at home plate to improve his swing and raise his batting average. As captain of the team, he helped Yale win the NCAA Eastern baseball championship in 1948.

Opposite page: Bush at Yale in his baseball uniform

Jamming his coursework into a two-and-a-half-year schedule, Bush graduated from Yale that spring. "Like other married veterans in the late 1940s," he recalled, "I was on a fast track to get my degree and make up for lost time." Already he and his wife had a baby son, George, Jr. At the age of twenty-four, Bush felt ready to start a career. "I was young in years but matured in outlook," he remembered. "The world I'd known before the war didn't interest me. I was looking for a different kind of life, something challenging, outside the established mold."

Rather than accept safe employment in his father's banking firm, Bush looked for work elsewhere. Wealthy family friend Neil Mallon suggested, "What you need to do is head out to Texas and those oil fields. That's the place for ambitious young people these days." As head of an oil-drilling equipment company called Dresser Industries, Mallon gave Bush a job. "You'll be an equipment clerk," he explained. "There's not much salary, but if you want to learn the oil business, it's a start."

Full of hope, Bush packed up his little family and headed for the dusty plains of western Texas. In the town of Odessa, they settled into half of a small, two-family house. Dresser Industries owned a company called Ideco (International Derrick and Equipment Company). At the Ideco store in Odessa, Bush gladly undertook every task given him, including painting oil pumps under the hot Texas sun. Working his way up to salesman, he sold Ideco drilling masts, derricks, casing, drill pipes, and tubing. Bush's fine work carried him for a time to California, where he sold drill bits, driving up and down the state

Bush (center) when he was president of Zapata Off-Shore drilling company

from oil rig to oil rig. "Robin, our first daughter, was born in Compton [California] in 1949," he remembered. "Beautiful hazel eyes, soft blond hair." When Dresser Industries next transferred Bush to Midland, Texas, he drove his growing family back to the Lone Star state.

The oil industry was booming in Midland in the early 1950s. As the price of oil swiftly rose, major oil companies and independent producers excitedly explored for new sources of crude oil. Getting caught up in the fever, Bush quit his Dresser Industries job in 1950. With a friend, John Overbey, he became an independent oil producer himself. Scouring the big cities, he found investors. Then he searched farmlands for places where oil might be hidden deep beneath the soil. The little Bush-Overbey Oil Development Company bought and sold oil-drilling royalty rights on parcels of land throughout the West.

"Bush-Overbey rocked along . . . ," John Overbey later recounted, "[and] somehow managed to stay in the black the entire three years of its existence." In 1953 Bush and Overbey merged their business with two other Texas friends, Bill and Hugh Leidtke. Together the men tried to decide upon a catchy name for their new company. The movie *Viva Zapata!*, starring Marlon Brando, was playing in downtown Midland just then. It was the story of the heroic Mexican rebel leader Emiliano Zapata. The partners quickly adopted the name. "And that's the way Zapata Petroleum was born," Bush declared.

Just as his new oil business began to prosper, tragedy struck the Bush family. Little Robin Bush grew weak and tired. "Your child has leukemia," their local doctor sadly revealed. The news that their daughter suffered from a deadly blood disease stunned the Bushes. Grasping for hope, they flew Robin to a hospital in New York for special treatment during the next six months.

"Spring passed into summer, summer into fall," remembered Bush. "Barbara stayed at the bedside; I shuttled between Midland and New York City." In time the strain took its toll on Barbara Bush. Almost overnight, her lovely brown hair turned white.

"Gradually but surely," Bush later mourned, "Robin slipped away. She was three years and ten months old when she died." "I nearly fell apart," grieved Barbara Bush. "I couldn't put my right foot in front of my left, but George didn't let me retreat." By then the Bushes had another little baby, Jeb. As they slowly overcame their sad loss, other children followed: Neil, Marvin, and Dorothy.

Bush and his young family in Texas

All the while, Zapata Petroleum continued to grow. "By the end of 1954 we had 71 wells producing an average of 1,250 barrels a day," recalled Bush. That year the company also began offshore drilling operations. On oil barges, rig drills cut deep into the sand beneath the Gulf of Mexico. Soon, precious oil discoveries made Zapata pumping stations at sea profitable.

As Zapata's success increased, Bush and his partners agreed to separate their onshore and offshore drilling operations. In 1959, Zapata Off-Shore became a separate company, with thirty-five-year-old George Bush as its president. Moving his headquarters and family to Houston, Texas, he undertook the difficult responsibility of running his new company. In time, successful Zapata Off-Shore drilling rigs dotted the coasts of five continents. By 1966 Bush's stock in Zapata was valued at a million dollars. His gamble in Texas had made him rich.

Above: Oilman Bush talks with a driller.
Opposite page: Running for congressman in 1966

BUSH

Chapter 4

"Bitten by the Bug"

"I'd helped build a company from the ground up," Bush explained. "Zapata Off-Shore was thriving. We had financial security, warm, close friends, and a comfortable home. I was still young, only in my thirties—young enough to look for new challenges."

In 1952 Prescott Bush had won election as a Republican U.S. senator from Connecticut. Through the next ten years he ably represented the people of his state in the Capitol's Senate chamber. Following his father's example, Bush developed a greater interest in politics starting in the early 1960s. Texas was a stronghold of the Democratic political party. Bush, however, dutifully took his place among the state's few Republicans. In 1963 the wealthy young oilman won his first political office, the chairmanship of Harris County's Republican Committee.

The next year Bush plunged much more deeply into politics. He challenged popular Texas Democrat Ralph Yarborough for his seat in the U.S. Senate. Through the next months Bush campaigned hard, meeting voters and discussing the issues. "Barbara and I . . . traveled Texas," he exclaimed, "from the Panhandle to the Rio Grande, Wichita Falls to Beeville. There's no better way to learn about the state [and] its people."

Opposite page: Bush as ambassador to the United Nations in 1971

Bush's parents, Dorothy and Senator Prescott Bush

The tough Senate race continued right up to election day. As a Republican, Bush realized he had little hope of winning. "Ralph wins in Texas Sweep," blared the *Houston Post* the next day. Even in defeat, however, Bush took satisfaction. He had piled up more votes and run a closer contest against his opponent than had any other Republican in Texas history.

Bush returned to his work at Zapata Off-Shore, but his secretary Aleene Smith noticed, "he just didn't have his

Bush and supporters during his Senate race

heart in making money any more." As Bush himself admitted, "the 1964 Senate race had a profound impact on my outlook on life." To a friend he confessed that he had been "bitten by the bug." In February 1966 Bush resigned as head of Zapata Off-Shore in order to run for Congress. "I remember asking him why the hell he was giving up all this to take some $18,000 a year job," stated Zapata vice-president L. V. Whittington. "I can't even explain it to my wife," answered Bush, "so how . . . am I supposed to explain it to you? But I've got big things in mind."

Watching election returns: George, father Prescott, and brother Jonathan

Bush sold his share in Zapata Off-Shore and started his race for the congressional seat in the newly formed Seventh District of Houston. Rolling up his sleeves, the forty-two-year-old candidate shook hands with voters and gave speeches. "ELECT GEORGE BUSH TO CONGRESS AND WATCH THE ACTION," exclaimed his campaign slogan. Impressed with his energy, on November 9, 1966, Houston-area voters elected him by a margin of 57 percent over his Democratic opponent. Congressman George Bush was on his way to Washington.

In January 1967, Bush took his oath of office at the Capitol. As an enthusiastic freshman member of the House of Representatives, the smiling Texan quickly made his mark. "He was one of our leaders," recalled Illinois congressman Tom Railsback. "If we had to pick one guy who

George and Barbara during his campaign for congressman

would have a bright future, it would have been George Bush." As a conservative Republican, Bush voted against lowering gasoline prices, and he supported the Vietnam War. His popularity in his home district won him reelection to a second two-year term in 1968.

Bush's liberal stand on civil rights issues angered some Houston citizens, however. New open-housing laws, which Bush supported, outraged local conservatives who wished to keep minorities out of their neighborhoods. Bravely Bush defended his beliefs before one jeering Houston crowd. "Somehow, it seems fundamental," he explained, "that a man—if he has money and the good character—should not have a door slammed in his face if he is a Negro or speaks with a Latin-American accent." Affected by the decency of his words, many listeners loudly applauded.

The Bushes celebrate victory in the 1966 congressional election.

The Bush family greatly enjoyed their time in Washington. The congressman's wife and children remained the most important part of Bush's life. Friends eagerly accepted invitations to attend the Bushes' regular Sunday barbecues. "Everyone always wanted to come over to our house," young Marvin Bush happily recalled. Cheerful family members and guests crowded the Bush yard, gobbling hamburgers and tossing horseshoes.

Republican president Richard Nixon admired Bush's work in Congress. In 1970 he urged the forty-six-year-old to run for the Senate again, this time against conservative Texan Lloyd Bentsen. Taking up the challenge, Bush campaigned hard from the cities to the prairies. "GEORGE BUSH—HE CAN DO MORE," promised his slogan. The Democrats countered with, "LLOYD BENTSEN—A COURAGEOUS TEXAN WITH FRESH IDEAS."

As election day approached, the *Houston Chronicle* declared, "Bentsen started the general election campaign a decided favorite . . . but all indications point to a neck-and-neck finish, with Bush closing fast." On the first Tuesday in November 1970, Texas voters walked to their polling places. Soon Bush learned of his defeat by 157,000 votes. "Who would have thought," exclaimed the *Chronicle*, "that Bush could get 1,033,243 votes and still lose?"

Although deeply disappointed by his political failure, within a month Bush sprang back with a new job. As a reward for his loyal Republican effort in Texas, President Nixon appointed him U.S. ambassador to the United Nations (UN).

Every year, UN delegates from over one hundred countries gathered in New York City to discuss and deal with issues of international importance. In March 1971 Bush strode into the United Nations General Assembly, eager to represent the interests of the United States.

Critics complained that Bush had no experience in foreign affairs. Soon the raging China question put the new ambassador's diplomatic skills to the test.

A revolution had brought Chinese communist leader Mao Zedong to power in 1949. As a result, millions of Nationalist Chinese, opposed to the communist government, had fled to the island of Taiwan. For years the United Nations had recognized Nationalist China as the rightful Chinese government. In October 1971, however, many small "Third World" nations demanded that Communist ("Red") China be admitted to the UN and Nationalist China be thrown out.

UN ambassador Bush casting a vote

Publicly, the United States stood with its Taiwanese ally. "We offer representation and a seat on the Security Council to Red China," Bush declared. "At the same time, we feel that Nationalist China . . . should continue to have representation in the UN." Through the next days the General Assembly debated the important issue. Witnesses marveled as Bush hurried from UN receptions to foreign missions to present his views to his fellow ambassadors. "Whatever George Bush lacked in diplomatic polish," exclaimed *Life* magazine afterwards, "he made up in wit, stamina and enthusiasm." One UN diplomat remarked, "You may dislike what George is trying to do, but you can't dislike George."

"It's a cliff-hanger," predicted Bush as the day for the vote arrived. American hopes hinged on making the Taiwan resolution an "important question," requiring a two-thirds majority vote to pass. By a very close vote of 59 to 55, the General Assembly refused. Unhappily Bush watched as the members afterwards kicked Taiwan out of the UN by a thumping vote of 76 to 35.

"For George Bush, who had lobbied for weeks to win votes for [Taiwan], it was both a defeat and a deep personal disappointment," reported *Life* magazine. "In trying to save Taiwan's seat, he had set what must be a UN track record for personal effort." "We came a long way," the UN ambassador wearily sighed, "but not long enough." As Red China took its place at the UN at the expense of Nationalist China, President Nixon officially recognized the communist government for the first time.

Following his successful reelection campaign in 1972, Nixon decided to make major changes in his administration. "George," he told Bush, ". . . the place I really need you is over at the National Committee running things." The chairmanship of the Republican National Committee failed to excite Bush very much. "When the President wants you to do something," he loyally remarked, however, "in my kind of civics, you ought to do it." In January 1973, he switched to a new office in Washington as head of the Republican Party.

During the next months, Bush's job to promote Republican causes grew difficult. First, a bribery scandal forced Vice-President Spiro Agnew to resign from office in October 1973. To take Agnew's place, Nixon chose House Minority Leader Gerald Ford.

Soon an even greater scandal rocked the White House. During the 1972 presidential race, political spies had been caught planting listening devices at the Democratic headquarters in Washington's Watergate office complex. Nixon's repeated attempts to cover up White House involvement in the shameful Watergate break-in enraged most Americans.

For a time, Republican chairman Bush tried to support Nixon. As the scandal widened and he learned the truth, however, his attitude changed. Traveling the country almost nonstop, Bush bolstered sagging Republican morale and gave speeches distancing the party from the growing mess in Washington. "It wasn't pleasant in those days to be party spokesman," one Republican coworker remembered. "But Bush did it with class and earned a lot of respect in the process."

By August 1974, continued investigations into the Watergate scandal caused the Senate to consider impeaching Nixon, forcing him from office. "Watergate was taking [the] President down," Bush realized. On August 7, 1974, the Republican chairman gravely wrote to Nixon: "Dear Mr. President, It is my considered judgment that you should now resign. . . ." Other Republican leaders also strongly advised the shaken president to spare the country and the Republican Party further turmoil.

Richard Nixon waves good-bye after his resignation.

Caving in to the pressure, Richard Nixon resigned on August 9, 1974. A broken man, he climbed aboard the presidential helicopter and left the White House. The historic scene affected Bush deeply. "As chairman of the Republican National Committee, I felt a tremendous load had been taken off my shoulders," he confessed, "but as a person who owed Richard Nixon a great deal . . . I was saddened by what I saw as not merely a political disaster but a human tragedy."

Chapter 5

Missions Abroad and at Home

"A political nightmare," Bush afterwards described his time as Republican National Committee chairman. The new president, Gerald Ford, highly valued Bush's efforts to hold the Republican Party together during that period.

Within days President Ford summoned Bush to the White House. "When I visited the Oval Office," Bush recalled, "the President . . . mentioned the fact that two key diplomatic posts were about to open up. Ambassador to Great Britain and Ambassador to France." Instead, Bush asked to be appointed head of the U.S. Liaison Office in China. "An important, coveted post like London or Paris would be good for the resume," he later explained, "but Beijing was a challenge, a journey into the unknown."

Leaving their children behind in school, in September 1974 George and Barbara Bush flew to China. At that time, the United States did not have formal diplomatic relations with the People's Republic of China, as it was now called. In fact, after twenty-five years of complete isolation, the great Asian nation was just beginning to open up to the West. Everything seemed new and strange to the Bushes as they settled into the Chinese capital at Beijing.

George and Barbara Bush in Beijing, China

"A veil of secrecy surrounded diplomatic life in China," Bush soon discovered. "As far as the Chinese were concerned, foreign visitors were in their country to learn only what their hosts wanted them to learn." As the United States carefully moved to restore normal relations with China, Secretary of State Henry Kissinger predicted that Bush would find his job stuffy and boring.

"Within a month," Bush zestfully exclaimed, however, "I took my first step in breaking the mold on what was expected from a U.S. envoy to Beijing." Instead of traveling about by sedan, Bush and his wife hopped on bicycles and pedaled through the streets along with thousands of

Chinese Communist Party chairman Mao Zedong

Chinese. With smiles, the Chinese staff at the U.S. Liaison Office soon described the couple as "Bushes, who ride the bicycle, just as the Chinese do."

Bush and his wife studied Chinese language and culture. They cheerfully attended receptions at the various foreign embassies in Beijing. In small and friendly ways, the ambassador strengthened America's role in China. Twice Secretary of State Kissinger visited China while Bush was there. Together they met with high Chinese officials. Finally allowed to meet the aging Chairman Mao Zedong himself, Bush guessed that full diplomatic relations with China soon would resume.

President Ford and Chinese vice-premier Teng review troops in Beijing.

In December 1975, President Ford journeyed to China. During another meeting, Chairman Mao greeted Bush with "You've been promoted." Turning to President Ford, he added, "We hate to see him go." One month earlier, Secretary of State Kissinger had sent an important cable to Bush from Washington: "THE PRESIDENT IS PLANNING TO ANNOUNCE SOME MAJOR PERSONNEL SHIFTS [AND] ASKS THAT YOU CONSENT TO HIS NOMINATING YOU AS THE NEW DIRECTOR OF THE CENTRAL INTELLIGENCE AGENCY. THE PRESIDENT FEELS YOUR APPOINTMENT TO BE GREATLY IN THE NATIONAL INTEREST AND VERY MUCH HOPES THAT YOU WILL ACCEPT."

Bush leaves Beijing for his post as CIA director.

It was a time of trouble for the Central Intelligence Agency (CIA). "I was being asked," recalled Bush, ". . . to return to Washington and take charge of an agency battered by a decade of hostile congressional investigations, exposés, and charges that ran from lawbreaking to simple incompetence." The demands of this new post also would prohibit Bush's Republican Party activities. The director of the CIA must never take sides on political issues. Still he agreed to accept the challenge. "Barbara and I left Beijing with mixed feelings," he confessed: "warm memories of our thirteen months in China, but glad to be going home; satisfied with the job we'd done, but looking down what appeared to be a political dead-end street."

In January 1976, Bush stepped into his new office at CIA headquarters in Langley, Virginia. "The agency's sole duty outlined in its 1947 charter," the new director explained, "is to furnish intelligence data to the President and other policy makers. . . . In the CIA an intelligence officer isn't a 'spy' in the popular cloak-and-dagger image, but an analyst in some special area—foreign politics, economics, military affairs, agriculture, to name a few."

Through the next months Director Bush worked hard to see that the agency performed within its chartered guidelines. "I'd usually be at my desk around seven-fifty," he revealed, "and spend the next half hour or so reviewing a summary of overnight cable traffic from CIA stations around the world. . . . Once a week . . . I'd report to the White House for an early-morning briefing session with President Ford."

Senate investigations into past CIA scandals brought Director Bush to Capitol Hill. In less than a year, he appeared before Congress an astonishing fifty-one times. His straightforward testimony eased public fears about many CIA secret activities.

In the fall of 1976, Democratic candidate Jimmy Carter of Georgia defeated Gerald Ford in the U.S. presidential election. As the new administration prepared to enter Washington, fifty-one-year-old Bush graciously offered to resign his office. "This job was well worth a year of my life," he announced as he packed his bags once more. "There's a certain luxury to beginning again. I don't know for sure [what I'll do next], but it's likely that I'll save some time for politics."

Above: President Jimmy Carter and Vice-President Walter Mondale
Below: Jimmy Carter takes his oath of office in January 1977.

President Reagan and Vice-President Bush

Chapter 6

A Heartbeat Away

Bush returned to Houston, where he worked as a consultant at First International Bancshares, the largest bank in Texas. Clearly he missed public life, though. As Jimmy Carter's Democratic administration seemed to proceed without direction, and the national economy faltered, Bush ambitiously considered running for president himself. "America needed soneone in the Oval Office who could restore the people's faith in our institutions," Bush later commented, "a leader who could revitalize the national spirit."

Longtime Texas friend James Baker agreed to help raise money for a political campaign. Through 1978 Bush traveled more than 92,000 miles in 42 states, making contacts, meeting Republican officials, and testing the political waters. "Bush is running early, often and hard—and with surprising success," revealed an article in a December *Newsweek* magazine. "With a pocket flight guide in his rumpled Brooks Brothers suit and carry-on luggage in hand, Bush just keeps running."

"Just who is this guy Bush?" asked a curious stewardess on an Alaska Airlines flight. "And what's he doing in Alaska?" Pursuing an exhausting and lonely schedule, Bush took his political message to the people. On May 1, 1979, he formally announced his campaign for the Republican presidential nomination. Through the next months the tireless candidate logged another 250,000 miles and attended a staggering 853 political events.

Well-known former California governor Ronald Reagan nearly had won the Republican nomination in 1976. Earnestly Bush undertook the task of beating the popular Reagan in 1980.

The race for delegates and support began in Iowa, the first state to hold a political caucus. "Winning early meant winning in Iowa," Bush declared. With startling enthusiasm Bush toured that state eleven times. "We owned Iowa over the summer," crowed campaign worker Rich Bond. "The other candidates were there, but we were the only ones hustling." "He's been everywhere," marveled Iowa Republican chairman Steven Roberts.

Audiences cheered Bush's patriotic speeches. "We are the most decent and honorable country that has ever come down the pike," he proclaimed to one crowd. "Sure, there are a lot of problems out there, but we can solve them." When opponents ridiculed Bush's cracking voice and sometimes dull speaking style, he responded straightforwardly, "Some others might be more exciting orators. But we're not trying to elect a class valedictorian; we're trying to elect somebody who can restore confidence in this country. . . ."

Republican Iowans—impressed by Bush's energy, his politics, and his national and foreign experience—walked to local caucus meetings on January 21, 1980. In a surprising upset they awarded Bush 31.5 percent of their votes. Front-runner Ronald Reagan received only 29.4 percent. Overnight Bush became a household name, the man to watch in the presidential race. Bush excitedly boasted that his campaign now had "Big Mo"—momentum!

Alarmed by Bush's Iowa victory, Reagan doubled his efforts in New Hampshire, the first state to hold a primary vote to elect convention delegates. Eagerly Reagan paid the expenses for a debate with Bush to be sponsored by a New Hampshire newspaper, the *Nashua Telegraph.* Local citizens jammed the Nashua High School auditorium on January 29, the night of the debate. In a surprise move, other Republican candidates showed up on the stage, wishing to take part in the discussion, too. Reagan thought that would be fair, but *Telegraph* editor Jon Breen tried to stop Reagan from expressing his opinion. The audience cheered as Reagan furiously grabbed his microphone and reminded Breen, "I am paying for this microphone!"

During this dramatic confrontation, Bush remained strangely uncommitted. "I will play by the rules, and I'm glad to be here," he simply stated. Afterwards he realized his mistake. "I could have handled certain things better," he admitted. Reagan's outspokenness that night and his fiery energy as he traveled the state gained him renewed support. As a result, on primary day, February 26, New Hampshire Republicans gave Reagan 50 percent of their votes. Bush came in second, receiving only 23 percent.

Bush campaigning in New Hampshire in 1980

Bush kept fighting, but his campaign clearly had lost its "Big Mo." Through the next months the Reagan bandwagon rolled through other primary states, gathering up hundreds of convention delegates. In his speeches, Reagan called for a radical plan to cut both government spending and income taxes to revive the economy. Bush ridiculed this program, calling it "voodoo economics." Although he scored successes in Pennsylvania, Michigan, and other large industrial states, Bush soon realized that Reagan was closing in on the 998 delegates needed for nomination. Finally, in June 1980, he admitted his defeat. "I'm an optimist," he announced, "but I also know how to count to 998."

Wearily Bush journeyed to the Republican national convention in Detroit, Michigan, in July. He wondered if his political career finally had reached its end. In the Joe Louis Arena, excited delegates roared, bands blared, and balloons dropped from the ceiling when the first ballot brought Reagan's official victory.

For a time Reagan tried to create what was called a "dream ticket," with ex-president Gerald Ford as his vice-presidential running mate. That plan fell through, though, when Ford demanded to share more presidential power than Reagan was willing to grant him. Hurriedly Reagan scrambled to find another popular, qualified running mate.

Sitting in his hotel room, Bush heard the sudden ringing of his telephone. "Hello, George, this is Ron Reagan," the familiar voice greeted him. After a pause Reagan revealed, "I'd like to go over to the convention and announce that you're my choice for Vice President . . . if that's all right with you."

"I'd be honored, Governor," Bush answered with happy surprise. When he hung up the telephone, he and his family hugged each other and shouted with excitement. That night, Republican conventioneers roared their approval of George Bush for vice-president.

In August, Democrats nominated Jimmy Carter to run for a second term at their convention in New York City. The delegates picked Walter Mondale of Minnesota to run again for vice-president. Unhappy with the choices of both parties, Illinois congressman John Anderson announced he would run for president as an independent candidate.

As the campaign began, Bush quickly showed his loyalty to Reagan's conservative brand of politics. He buried his philosophical differences and fully joined the Reagan team. The two Republicans canvassed the countryside appealing to the people for votes.

Democrats joked about Reagan's past as a motion-picture actor. In fact, his acting career proved very helpful. Bush admired Reagan's poised and witty speaking skills in interviews and speeches. In a television debate with Jimmy Carter, Reagan swayed the opinions of millions of viewers. "Are you better off," he simply asked them, "than you were four years ago?"

By election day, November 4, 1980, Americans clearly had decided they wanted a change. Carter admitted defeat even before some polling places had closed. When the votes were finally counted they revealed:

	Popular Vote	Electoral Vote
Ronald Reagan	43,899,248	489
Jimmy Carter	35,481,435	49
John Anderson	5,719,437	0

By a huge margin, Americans had elected the Reagan-Bush team. In Houston, Bush celebrated with his family and excitedly looked forward to the challenges of his newest job.

On inauguration day, January 20, 1981, thousands of people waved flags and packed the streets of Washington, D.C. Near the west front of the Capitol, citizens eagerly jammed shoulder-to-shoulder to witness the swearing-in ceremonies. Just after noon on that clear, crisp day, fifty-six-year-old George Bush stepped across the platform.

Bush takes the vice-presidential oath of office in January 1981.

Raising his hand, he solemnly repeated the oath of the vice-president of the United States, administered by his friend Supreme Court Justice Potter Stewart. Soon after, Reagan swore his presidential oath and turned to deliver his inaugural address. The new vice-president joined in the crowd's applause as Reagan promised to make the national government work again.

Many people considered the vice-presidency to be an unimportant job. Bush's only official duty, as outlined in the U.S. Constitution, was to preside over the Senate and to break tied votes in that chamber. Eagerly, however, he looked for extra work to do. "I'm not going to be totally invisible," he told one newsman. "My role will be to have the confidence of the President. . . . I owe the President my judgment as well as my loyalty."

President Reagan, seconds after being shot outside the Washington Hilton

In office just seventy days, on March 30, 1981, the vice-president faced his first major crisis. While flying to Austin, Texas, to deliver a speech, Bush received a shocking message: President Reagan had been shot outside the Hilton Hotel in Washington, D.C. Newsmen had captured the terrible event on film. Bush quickly switched on the government airplane's television and watched. He saw "the President smiling and waving before he stepped into his car, the crack of gunfire, people hitting the pavement, Secret Service agents struggling with the suspect [crazed drifter John Hinckley, Jr.], the President's car speeding away." Soon he learned that Reagan was undergoing dangerous emergency surgery for a bullet wound in the chest. Three other men also had been wounded in the attack: Secret Service agent Tim McCarthy, Washington police officer Thomas Delahanty, and White House press secretary James Brady.

"We're going to refuel in Austin and go back," Bush instantly ordered. As his plane soared back to Washington, Bush learned that the president had survived his surgery. Doctors at George Washington University Hospital had removed the bullet from Reagan's left lung. Still, the shooting shocked and frightened many Americans. The government seemed leaderless and in total confusion. Soon, at a White House press conference, Vice-President Bush calmed all fears. "The American government is functioning fully and effectively," he insisted.

Through the next tense days, Bush ably filled in for the president at nearly every official White House function. His low-key, steady conduct and his clear respect for Reagan greatly impressed many White House workers. The White House chief of staff, Bush's old friend James Baker, remarked, "He is performing extremely well. He's filling in for the President without being brash or overly assertive." Meeting regularly with the cabinet and the U.S. National Security Council, Bush helped guide government policy while the president recovered.

Americans cheered Reagan's release from the hospital on April 11. Gladly Bush greeted his boss's return to duty, too. "It never occurred to me even for a fleeting moment that I was anything more than a stand-in," the vice-president remarked. The awful assassination attempt, however, reminded him that he was just one heartbeat away from being president. "The whole thing brings it home," he declared. "I don't dwell on it—but I guess it's there."

Moved by Bush's loyalty and proven work record, Reagan sought the advice of his vice-president more often. "I have plenty of opportunities to chat privately with the President," Bush soon revealed. Usually the two men lunched together on Thursdays in the Oval Office. "There was no formal agenda," the vice-president remembered. "The lunches were relaxed, the conversation wide-ranging, from affairs of state to small talk."

"Stay busy and keep quiet," reported a *U.S. News & World Report* story. "That's the method George Bush is employing to back up the President in handling issues at home and abroad." Following a hectic schedule, Bush zigzagged across the nation giving speeches at Republican fund-raising events. To spread American goodwill, the vice-president traveled to fifty-nine foreign countries on behalf of the Reagan administration.

Bush also headed special commissions for the president. As head of the Task Force for Regulatory Relief, he recommended ways to cut paperwork in government agencies. Another Bush task force sought to stop illegal drug smuggling in south Florida. Coordinating the efforts of the Pentagon, the Coast Guard, and local police, Bush worked to curb the flow of drugs into the country.

Under Reagan's economic policies, American businesses boomed during his four-year term. Called the Great Communicator, Reagan saw his popularity soar. As the 1984 national election approached, Bush gladly rejoined Reagan on the Republican campaign ticket. In August 1984, Republican delegates gathered in Dallas, Texas, where Reagan and Bush unanimously won renomination.

Democratic candidates Walter Mondale and Geraldine Ferraro

Earlier at their July convention in San Francisco, California, cheering Democrats awarded their party's nomination to former vice-president Walter Mondale. Mondale realized he would have trouble winning in November. To startle voters and attract greater interest in the campaign, he picked New York congresswoman Geraldine Ferraro as his vice-presidential running mate. No major U.S. political party ever had chosen a woman for its national ticket before.

Still, the Reagan-Bush team seemed unbeatable. Through the summer Bush campaigned hard on behalf of the Republican ticket. Some Democrats complained that Bush supported the president too completely. "One thing about Bush—he's not a yes-man," teased one 1984 campaign joke. "If Reagan says, 'No,' he says 'No!' too."

The two vice-presidential candidates debate in Philadelphia.

For Bush, the highlight of the 1984 campaign occurred in October. "Shoot-Out at the Gender Gap," *Newsweek* magazine called it. The "shoot-out" was Bush's nationally televised debate with Geraldine Ferraro. For eighty-five minutes the two vice-presidential candidates discussed campaign issues. Bush stressed his obvious experience in national and foreign affairs, while Ferraro proved a capable speaker. In the end, most people agreed that Bush had won the hard-fought debate.

Through the last days of the election race, the candidates blazed the campaign trail. Most Americans felt sure that Reagan and Bush would be impossible to beat. On November 7, 1984, citizens headed for the polls to cast their ballots. The final tally showed:

	Popular Vote	Electoral Vote
Ronald Reagan	54,450,603	525
Walter Mondale	37,575,671	13

In the Capitol rotunda on January 21, 1985, the sixty-year-old politician swore his oath for a second time.

"I can't wait to get to work every day," the veteran vice-president announced with enthusiasm. "I've got plenty to do, and I feel comfortable in my job." On typical days Bush arrived at his White House office by 7:00 A.M. and received briefings and reports. Through the day he usually attended cabinet meetings and the conferences of the White House staff. As president of the Senate, Bush's duties sometimes called him to the Capitol. By 7:00 P.M. the vice-president's workday usually ended. Seated in his limousine, he traveled through Washington's streets to the sixteen-room vice-presidential mansion on the grounds of the nearby U.S. Naval Observatory.

Often George and Barbara entertained guests at dinner. Standing six feet, two inches tall, the handsome, blue-eyed vice-president always greeted company with friendly smiles and warm handshakes. For exercise Bush regularly jogged outdoors or used a running machine. Still swinging his racket with speed and skill, he liked playing tennis whenever possible.

Bush clearly enjoyed hardy health. Many Americans worried, however, about President Reagan's health. The oldest president in United States history, Reagan already had survived a bullet in the chest. In July 1985, the seventy-four-year-old president faced a second important personal battle. During a medical exam, doctors discovered a tumor two inches long growing on his large intestine. "The President has cancer," gravely announced Dr. Steven Rosenberg.

Reagan needed surgery to remove a two-foot section of his large intestine. To avoid national confusion and fears during the operation, the president decided to invoke the Twenty-Fifth Amendment to the U.S. Constitution for the second time in history. That 1967 amendment provided for the filling of vacancies in the offices of president and vice-president. (The amendment was first invoked in 1973, when Vice-President Spiro Agnew resigned and was replaced by Gerald Ford.)

On July 13, Reagan lay in Bethesda Naval Medical Center in Maryland and signed the document transferring presidential power to Bush. "I have determined and it is my . . . direction that Vice-President George Bush shall discharge [presidential] powers and duties in my stead, commencing with the administration of anesthesia to me." At 11:28 A.M., doctors rendered Reagan unconscious and began the operation. At that moment George Bush formally became acting president of the United States.

Through the day, Bush performed the routine duties of the president. One Bush aide later reported, "We wanted it seen that the Vice-President and others were simply in place, doing their jobs calmly."

After a full day of successful surgery, doctors at last allowed Reagan to regain consciousness. Once again alert, at 7:22 P.M. the president signed a second letter reclaiming his power and duties. Through the next week, while Reagan recovered at the hospital, Bush ran the nation's daily business. When Reagan finally returned, Bush stood among those most happy to welcome him back to the White House.

Bush visits Reagan in the hospital.

The friendship of the two men had grown stronger over the years. "He's a solid team player," said one of Reagan's aides about Bush. As the Reagan administration progressed, Bush advised the president on a number of important issues. "I like the satisfaction of just walking down the hall and telling the President what I think," he told one newsman.

Oliver North and his attorney, Brendan Sullivan, during the Iran-contra hearings

In 1987, though, the Iran-contra scandal broke, and some Americans angrily wondered what part Bush had played in the affair. Against stated national policy, the White House secretly had traded weapons to the Middle Eastern country of Iran. In exchange, Reagan had hoped to win the freedom of several American hostages being held by Middle Eastern terrorists. To make matters worse, profits from the weapons sale had gone to Central America to help rebel soldiers called "contras" fight the communist troops of Nicaragua's Sandinista government. This defied a law passed by Congress in 1984.

Americans roared with fury and Washington buzzed with questions about the Iran-contra scandal. Both a special commission and a congressional committee launched investigations into the affair. The Tower Com-

Oliver North is sworn in before testifying about his contra aid activities.

mission discovered that U.S. Marine colonel Oliver North, a staff member of the National Security Council, had run the illegal contra aid operation. In a national apology, President Reagan accepted responsibility for not preventing the scandal. Like Reagan, Vice-President Bush claimed he had known nothing about North's activities.

Americans could not stay mad at the popular president for long. The many triumphs of the Reagan years easily overshadowed the failures. The national economy thrived, and U.S. citizens felt a deeper patriotic pride under Reagan's leadership than they had felt in many years. In addition, improved relations with the Soviet Union offered the promise of international peace. Vice-President Bush could review his contributions during these years with a real sense of satisfaction.

Chapter 7

The Road to the White House

Vice-President Martin Van Buren had been elected U.S. president in 1836. In the 152 years since then, no sitting vice-president ever had gone on to win the highest office in the land. After faithfully serving in the Reagan administration, though, George Bush believed his time had come. As the 1988 national campaign season began, he announced his desire to run for president. "He's discharged his responsibility to Ronald Reagan and he's going into business for himself," remarked Texas politician Robert Strauss.

Other Republicans also sought the nomination. They attacked front-runner Bush at every opportunity, claiming he lacked the personality and independence required of a president. Richard Wirthlin, a pollster for Kansas senator Robert Dole, remarked, "There's just something about Bush that bothers me. Maybe he's a wimp."

Opposite page: Bush throws out the first pitch in a New York Mets/Montreal Expos game.

Hurt and angered by this name-calling, Bush toughened his campaign. During a live television interview, CBS newsman Dan Rather rudely questioned Bush's role during the Iran-contra scandal. "It's not fair to judge my whole career by a rehash on Iran," counterattacked the vice-president. "How would you like it if I judged your career by those seven minutes when you walked off the set in New York?" He referred to a recent embarrassment Rather had caused CBS. During an argument the newsman had stomped off the set, leaving the broadcast in an awkward blackout.

Bush's strong showing on television that night failed to sway many voters in Iowa's early caucus, though. On February 8, 1988, they awarded Senator Robert Dole 38 percent of their votes, while Bush trailed far behind with only 19 percent. "I guess we've got to get more of me out there," he told campaign aides in the wake of his defeat. Moving on to New Hampshire, he daily threw his suit coat aside and waded in among the people. Trading greetings and shaking hands, he showed his fighting spirit.

Bush supporters shouted with glee when New Hampshire citizens responded on primary day. The vice-president led the field with 38 percent of the vote. Stunned by the upset, the campaigns of Dole and other Republican contenders stalled. In March Bush scored huge victories in the primaries of a number of southern states. "A clean sweep. A shutout. It doesn't get any better than this," exclaimed his campaign manager, Lee Atwater. By late spring Bush had secured enough delegates to lock up the Republican presidential nomination.

Democratic candidates Michael Dukakis (center) and Lloyd Bentsen and their wives

At their July convention in Atlanta, the Democrats asked "Where was George?" as they reviewed the faults of the Reagan years. Finally they selected Massachusetts governor Michael Dukakis as their candidate. In a rousing acceptance speech, Dukakis called for honest government and national change. For his vice-presidential running mate, Dukakis picked Bush's old political rival, Texas senator Lloyd Bentsen. Polls taken after the exciting convention showed Dukakis leading Bush by a 17-percentage-point margin.

In August Republicans journeyed to New Orleans, Louisiana, for their convention. On August 17, Texas senator Phil Gramm placed Bush's name in nomination. "From naval aviator to Vice President," Gramm exclaimed, "George Bush . . . has never failed to answer his nation's call for service." Cheering Republican delegates unanimously chose Bush for president.

Bush listens as Dan Quayle answers a question at a news conference.

Bush selected J. Danforth Quayle to be his vice-presidential running mate. "You are my first and only choice," he told the forty-one-year-old senator from Indiana. Bush gambled that Dan Quayle's youth, good looks, and conservative politics would appeal to many voters. News reporters quickly discovered, however, that Quayle's college record had been weak and his performance in Congress lackluster. They also pounced upon the fact that, during the Vietnam War, Quayle had served safely in the Indiana National Guard while other young men endured combat. As the media attacked Quayle's personal history, many people questioned Bush's judgment in choosing him.

The Republican ticket seemed in trouble on August 18, as Bush crossed the podium to deliver his acceptance speech. "I mean to win," he sincerely declared. "I seek the

Bush takes a campaign jog through Chicago's Grant Park in August 1988.

Presidency to build a better America. It's that simple, and that big." Speaking of America's goodness, he called the nation's many voluntary organizations "a brilliant [mixture] spread like stars, like a thousand points of light in a broad and peaceful sky."

Delegates wildly cheered as Bush vowed not to raise federal taxes. "Congress will push me to raise taxes," he firmly exclaimed, ". . . And I'll say to them, read my lips: No New Taxes!" Speaking of the future, he touched his audience again by promising "a kinder, gentler nation." "I may sometimes be a little awkward," he admitted, "but there's nothing self-conscious in my love of country. . . . I'm a quiet man, but I hear the quiet people others don't—the ones who raise the family, pay the taxes, meet the mortgage. And I hear them and I am moved. . . ."

Bush and Quayle at a campaign rally in New Orleans, August 1988

Bush's heartfelt speech greatly affected millions of Americans. Overnight his chances of defeating Dukakis improved. "I will outwork him, outhustle him, outrun him, and outknowledge him," Bush insisted. "He has his strengths, but one of them isn't wanting to be President more than I do."

In addition to no new taxes, Bush pledged to balance the federal budget and create thirty million new American jobs. If elected, he promised to work toward further cuts in stockpiles of U.S. and Soviet nuclear missiles. He expressed a desire to become "the Education President" by spending more for new school programs. He also vowed to clamp down on drug pushers and other criminals.

Bush campaigners tore into Dukakis's record as Massachusetts governor. The state had become "Taxachusetts" while Dukakis sat in the governor's chair, they claimed. The pollution in Boston Harbor was blamed on him as well. On another front, a prisoner named Willie Horton who escaped while on a Massachusetts furlough program had committed other ugly crimes before his recapture. Surely, Bush staffers charged, this showed Dukakis was weak on crime.

The Republicans labeled Dukakis a far-left liberal and questioned his patriotism. As the mud-slinging continued, Dukakis fought back, accusing his opponent of "dragging the truth into the gutter." In television advertisements and on news programs the Democrats, in turn, smeared Bush's record.

Twice the two candidates met for televised debates. On September 25 they stood at lecterns at Wake Forest University in Winston-Salem, North Carolina. While Dukakis behaved with frosty seriousness, Bush sometimes seemed awkward when he spoke. After one verbal slip, Bush laughed at himself. "Wouldn't it be nice to be the Ice Man, so you never make a mistake?" Afterwards Republicans named the campaign a contest between the Nice Man (Bush) and the Ice Man (Dukakis).

After the debate Bush confessed to campaign aides, "I didn't do very well. I missed some opportunities." Looking forward, he promised, "Don't worry. I'll do better next time." Through the next days he campaigned vigorously, giving speeches and meeting the people. Each day, too, he spent time practicing his debating style.

Bush and Dukakis debate in Los Angeles.

On October 13 the two presidential candidates shook hands again, this time at the University of California in Los Angeles. Much more relaxed and confident, Bush responded to questions with steady charm and command. At the same time, Dukakis showed little emotion, reciting responses "as grimly as a schoolboy eating broccoli," commented *Newsweek* magazine. ". . . Bush . . . at least showed some human warmth. . . ." In the battle of personalities, it seemed Bush was beating Dukakis.

"Watch my smile . . . watch how fast we go—we're not letting up," exclaimed Bush as election day approached. Following his success in the second debate, he surged ahead in the polls. Desperately Dukakis barnstormed the nation, taking his message to the people. On election day, November 8, 1988, Bush Republicans still worried that their candidate might not win.

George and Barbara Bush watching election returns with their grandchildren

Bush returned to Houston, Texas, to vote. "Every time I vote here, I feel nervous," he admitted to reporters, ". . . but we are keeping our fingers crossed." Throughout the day American voters cast their ballots all across the country. A nearly complete tally of the votes soon showed the following results:

	Popular Vote	Electoral Vote
George Bush	47,946,422	426
Michael Dukakis	41,016,429	112

That night joyous Republicans celebrated everywhere. George Bush's long career of dedicated public service had earned him the nation's highest office. After a hard-fought campaign he had reached his lifetime goal. "The people have spoken," he afterwards declared. "With a full heart and great hopes, I thank all the people throughout America who have given us this great victory."

Chapter 8

"A New Breeze Is Blowing"

"When I said I wanted a kinder, gentler nation, I meant it—I mean it," sixty-four-year-old George Bush announced after his near-landslide election. Offering his friendship to those who had not supported him, he explained, "My hand is out to you and I want to be your president, too."

In the months leading to his inauguration, Americans wondered what kind of president Bush would be. "Having proved he can win a rough-and-tumble election," *Time* magazine remarked, "Bush must now prove he can manage the nation's . . . problems. . . ." During the Reagan years, the national debt had mushroomed to dangerous proportions. "If it wasn't for this deficit looming over everything," admitted Bush, "I'd feel like a spring colt." "We have to sit down with Congress and hammer out a budget-deficit agreement," he concluded. "There's lots of work to do." As Bush prepared for the days ahead, he named the people he wanted in his cabinet. Foremost among them was his valued old Texas friend James Baker, whom he appointed secretary of state.

After living eight years in the shadow of Ronald and Nancy Reagan, the Bushes soon would be moving into the White House. Eagerly Americans tried to learn everything they could about the new first family. People soon grew to admire George and Barbara Bush's close relationship and strong marriage. "I couldn't live without her, and she couldn't live without me," Bush lovingly revealed.

Fondly nicknamed "The Silver Fox" by her family, sixty-three-year-old Barbara Bush made no secret of her white hair or her age. "I'm so old now that I don't have to pretend to be something I'm not," she honestly declared. Her down-to-earth habits and well-bred grace quickly won the hearts of Americans. As honorary chairman of the Leukemia Society of America, she still worked to help find a cure for the disease that killed her little daughter.

She also promised to continue her long-standing fight against illiteracy in the United States. "If we can get people to read," she explained, "we can get them out of jails and shelters and off the streets and get them back to work." At the vice-presidential mansion she busily packed boxes. "George and I have lived in twenty-eight houses in seventeen cities in forty years," she marveled. Still she looked forward to moving to 1600 Pennsylvania Avenue.

George Bush often claimed that the greatest success of his life was that his children "still come home." Americans now braced themselves for a delightful Bush-family invasion of the White House. The five married Bush children would soon be exploring the wonders of the mansion. The ten Bush grandchildren would be running and playing in the halls. With enthusiasm, the president-

President Bush enjoying a game of tennis

elect announced his plan to put a horseshoe pit on the White House lawn.

Bush still expected to spend his summers at Walker's Point in Kennebunkport, Maine. Playing tennis, deep-sea fishing, or roaring through the ocean spray in his 28-foot speedboat, *Fidelity*, would offer the new president chances for relaxation.

As the days leading to his inauguration dwindled, Bush looked back over his full life. He recalled all the presidents he had known and served. He remembered his joys and struggles, his many political battles, and the difficult jobs he had held. Now with excitement and energy, he readied himself for his next great task.

The new president and his wife wave to well-wishers.

Inauguration day, January 20, 1989, dawned clear and cold in Washington, D.C. Before the flag-decked west front of the Capitol, thousands of citizens pressed close to watch the swearing-in ceremonies. On the crowded inaugural platform President Reagan, congressional leaders, and Bush family members, including Bush's eighty-seven-year-old mother, expectantly waited. Just after noon, George Bush stepped out at last to take the oath of office. This year, 1989, marked the two-hundredth anniversary of the first U.S. inauguration. Symbolically Bush placed his left hand upon two Bibles: the Bush family Bible and the Bible used by George Washington at his inauguration. Raising his right hand, he then slowly repeated the oath administered by Supreme Court chief justice William H.

Barbara smiles as George takes the oath of office.

Rehnquist. Swearing to "preserve, protect and defend" the Constitution, George Bush became forty-first president of the United States.

Cannons blasted a twenty-one-gun salute and the thrilled spectators cheered as he turned to deliver his inaugural address. "We meet on democracy's front porch," his voice proclaimed. "I come before you and assume the Presidency at a moment rich with promise. . . . A new breeze is blowing—and a nation refreshed by freedom stands ready to push on. . . . The American people await action . . . and tomorrow the work begins. And I do not mistrust the future; I do not fear what is ahead. For our problems are large, but our heart is larger. Our challenges are great, but our will is greater. . . ."

Reagan salutes back to Bush before boarding his helicopter.

Following his speech, the Bushes walked Ronald and Nancy Reagan to a waiting helicopter. The Reagans climbed aboard to leave Washington after eight long years. With a final sharp and respectful salute, President Bush wished ex-President Reagan a touching farewell.

The Reagan era was ending. The Bush years were about to begin. In the presidential limousine George and Barbara Bush started down Pennsylvania Avenue. Twice along the route the couple got out and walked. With broad smiles George Bush waved to the excited bystanders. With a springing step he moved ahead. To the cheering crowds it seemed that truly "a new breeze" was blowing. A new and hopeful United States president was on his way to the White House.

Opposite page: The inaugural ball

PRESIDENT AND
Bob Hardwick

Chronology of American History

(Shaded area covers events in George Bush's lifetime.)

About A.D. 982—Eric the Red, born in Norway, reaches Greenland in one of the first European voyages to North America.

About 1000—Leif Ericson (Eric the Red's son) leads what is thought to be the first European expedition to mainland North America; Leif probably lands in Canada.

1492—Christopher Columbus, seeking a sea route from Spain to the Far East, discovers the New World.

1497—John Cabot reaches Canada in the first English voyage to North America.

1513—Ponce de Léon explores Florida in search of the fabled Fountain of Youth.

1519-1521—Hernando Cortés of Spain conquers Mexico.

1534—French explorers led by Jacques Cartier enter the Gulf of St. Lawrence in Canada.

1540—Spanish explorer Francisco Coronado begins exploring the American Southwest, seeking the riches of the mythical Seven Cities of Cibola.

1565—St. Augustine, Florida, the first permanent European town in what is now the United States, is founded by the Spanish.

1607—Jamestown, Virginia, is founded, the first permanent English town in the present-day U.S.

1608—Frenchman Samuel de Champlain founds the village of Quebec, Canada.

1609—Henry Hudson explores the eastern coast of present-day U.S. for the Netherlands; the Dutch then claim parts of New York, New Jersey, Delaware, and Connecticut and name the area New Netherland.

1619—The English colonies' first shipment of black slaves arrives in Jamestown.

1620—English Pilgrims found Massachusetts' first permanent town at Plymouth.

1621—Massachusetts Pilgrims and Indians hold the famous first Thanksgiving feast in colonial America.

1623—Colonization of New Hampshire is begun by the English.

1624—Colonization of present-day New York State is begun by the Dutch at Fort Orange (Albany).

1625—The Dutch start building New Amsterdam (now New York City).

1630—The town of Boston, Massachusetts, is founded by the English Puritans.

1633—Colonization of Connecticut is begun by the English.

1634—Colonization of Maryland is begun by the English.

1636—Harvard, the colonies' first college, is founded in Massachusetts. Rhode Island colonization begins when Englishman Roger Williams founds Providence.

1638—Delaware colonization begins as Swedes build Fort Christina at present-day Wilmington.

1640—Stephen Daye of Cambridge, Massachusetts prints *The Bay Psalm Book*, the first English-language book published in what is now the U.S.

1643—Swedish settlers begin colonizing Pennsylvania.

About 1650—North Carolina is colonized by Virginia settlers.

1660—New Jersey colonization is begun by the Dutch at present-day Jersey City.

1670—South Carolina colonization is begun by the English near Charleston.

1673—Jacques Marquette and Louis Jolliet explore the upper Mississippi River for France.

1682—Philadelphia, Pennsylvania, is settled. La Salle explores Mississippi River all the way to its mouth in Louisiana and claims the whole Mississippi Valley for France.

1693—College of William and Mary is founded in Williamsburg, Virginia.

1700—Colonial population is about 250,000.

1703—Benjamin Franklin is born in Boston.

1732—George Washington, first president of the U.S., is born in Westmoreland County, Virginia.

1733—James Oglethorpe founds Savannah, Georgia; Georgia is established as the thirteenth colony.

1735—John Adams, second president of the U.S., is born in Braintree, Massachusetts.

1737—William Byrd founds Richmond, Virginia.

1738—British troops are sent to Georgia over border dispute with Spain.

1739—Black insurrection takes place in South Carolina.

1740—English Parliament passes act allowing naturalization of immigrants to American colonies after seven-year residence.

1743—Thomas Jefferson is born in Albemarle County, Virginia. Benjamin Franklin retires at age thirty-seven to devote himself to scientific inquiries and public service.

1744—King George's War begins; France joins war effort against England.

1745—During King George's War, France raids settlements in Maine and New York.

1747—Classes begin at Princeton College in New Jersey.

1748—The Treaty of Aix-la-Chapelle concludes King George's War.

1749—Parliament legally recognizes slavery in colonies and the inauguration of the plantation system in the South. George Washington becomes the surveyor for Culpepper County in Virginia.

1750—Thomas Walker passes through and names Cumberland Gap on his way toward Kentucky region. Colonial population is about 1,200,000.

1751—James Madison, fourth president of the U.S., is born in Port Conway, Virginia. English Parliament passes Currency Act, banning New England colonies from issuing paper money. George Washington travels to Barbados.

1752—Pennsylvania Hospital, the first general hospital in the colonies, is founded in Philadelphia. Benjamin Franklin uses a kite in a thunderstorm to demonstrate that lightning is a form of electricity.

1753—George Washington delivers command that the French withdraw from the Ohio River Valley; French disregard the demand. Colonial population is about 1,328,000.

1754—French and Indian War begins (extends to Europe as the Seven Years' War). Washington surrenders at Fort Necessity.

1755—French and Indians ambush Braddock. Washington becomes commander of Virginia troops.

1756—England declares war on France.

1758—James Monroe, fifth president of the U.S., is born in Westmoreland County, Virginia.

1759—Cherokee Indian war begins in southern colonies; hostilities extend to 1761. George Washington marries Martha Dandridge Custis.

1760—George III becomes king of England. Colonial population is about 1,600,000.

1762—England declares war on Spain.

1763—Treaty of Paris concludes the French and Indian War and the Seven Years' War. England gains Canada and most other French lands east of the Mississippi River.

1764—British pass the Sugar Act to gain tax money from the colonists. The issue of taxation without representation is first introduced in Boston. John Adams marries Abigail Smith.

1765—Stamp Act goes into effect in the colonies. Business virtually stops as almost all colonists refuse to use the stamps.

1766—British repeal the Stamp Act.

1767—John Quincy Adams, sixth president of the U.S. and son of second president John Adams, is born in Braintree, Massachusetts. Andrew Jackson, seventh president of the U.S., is born in Waxhaw settlement, South Carolina.

1769—Daniel Boone sights the Kentucky Territory.

1770—In the Boston Massacre, British soldiers kill five colonists and injure six. Townshend Acts are repealed, thus eliminating all duties on imports to the colonies except tea.

1771—Benjamin Franklin begins his autobiography, a work that he will never complete. The North Carolina assembly passes the "Bloody Act," which makes rioters guilty of treason.

1772—Samuel Adams rouses colonists to consider British threats to self-government.

1773—English Parliament passes the Tea Act. Colonists dressed as Mohawk Indians board British tea ships and toss 342 casks of tea into the water in what becomes known as the Boston Tea Party. William Henry Harrison is born in Charles City County, Virginia.

1774—British close the port of Boston to punish the city for the Boston Tea Party. First Continental Congress convenes in Philadelphia.

1775—American Revolution begins with battles of Lexington and Concord, Massachusetts. Second Continental Congress opens in Philadelphia. George Washington becomes commander-in-chief of the Continental army.

1776—Declaration of Independence is adopted on July 4.

1777—Congress adopts the American flag with thirteen stars and thirteen stripes. John Adams is sent to France to negotiate peace treaty.

1778—France declares war against Great Britain and becomes U.S. ally.

1779—British surrender to Americans at Vincennes. Thomas Jefferson is elected governor of Virginia. James Madison is elected to the Continental Congress.

1780—Benedict Arnold, first American traitor, defects to the British.

1781—Articles of Confederation go into effect. Cornwallis surrenders to George Washington at Yorktown, ending the American Revolution.

1782—American commissioners, including John Adams, sign peace treaty with British in Paris. Thomas Jefferson's wife, Martha, dies. Martin Van Buren is born in Kinderhook, New York.

1784—Zachary Taylor is born near Barboursville, Virginia.

1785—Congress adopts the dollar as the unit of currency. John Adams is made minister to Great Britain. Thomas Jefferson is appointed minister to France.

1786—Shays's Rebellion begins in Massachusetts.

1787—Constitutional Convention assembles in Philadelphia, with George Washington presiding; U.S. Constitution is adopted. Delaware, New Jersey, and Pennsylvania become states.

1788—Virginia, South Carolina, New York, Connecticut, New Hampshire, Maryland, and Massachusetts become states. U.S. Constitution is ratified. New York City is declared U.S. capital.

1789—Presidential electors elect George Washington and John Adams as first president and vice-president. Thomas Jefferson is appointed secretary of state. North Carolina becomes a state. French Revolution begins.

1790—Supreme Court meets for the first time. Rhode Island becomes a state. First national census in the U.S. counts 3,929,214 persons. John Tyler is born in Charles City County, Virginia.

1791—Vermont enters the Union. U.S. Bill of Rights, the first ten amendments to the Constitution, goes into effect. District of Columbia is established. James Buchanan is born in Stony Batter, Pennsylvania.

1792—Thomas Paine publishes *The Rights of Man.* Kentucky becomes a state. Two political parties are formed in the U.S., Federalist and Republican. Washington is elected to a second term, with Adams as vice-president.

1793—War between France and Britain begins; U.S. declares neutrality. Eli Whitney invents the cotton gin; cotton production and slave labor increase in the South.

1794—Eleventh Amendment to the Constitution is passed, limiting federal courts' power. "Whiskey Rebellion" in Pennsylvania protests federal whiskey tax. James Madison marries Dolley Payne Todd.

1795—George Washington signs the Jay Treaty with Great Britain. Treaty of San Lorenzo, between U.S. and Spain, settles Florida boundary and gives U.S. right to navigate the Mississippi. James Polk is born near Pineville, North Carolina.

1796—Tennessee enters the Union. Washington gives his Farewell Address, refusing a third presidential term. John Adams is elected president and Thomas Jefferson vice-president.

1797—Adams recommends defense measures against possible war with France. Napoleon Bonaparte and his army march against Austrians in Italy. U.S. population is about 4,900,000.

1798—Washington is named commander-in-chief of the U.S. Army. Department of the Navy is created. Alien and Sedition Acts are passed. Napoleon's troops invade Egypt and Switzerland.

1799—George Washington dies at Mount Vernon, New York. James Monroe is elected governor of Virginia. French Revolution ends. Napoleon becomes ruler of France.

1800—Thomas Jefferson and Aaron Burr tie for president. U.S. capital is moved from Philadelphia to Washington, D.C. The White House is built as presidents' home. Spain returns Louisiana to France. Millard Fillmore is born in Locke, New York.

1801—After thirty-six ballots, House of Representatives elects Thomas Jefferson president, making Burr vice-president. James Madison is named secretary of state.

1802—Congress abolishes excise taxes. U.S. Military Academy is founded at West Point, New York.

1803—Ohio enters the Union. Louisiana Purchase treaty is signed with France, greatly expanding U.S. territory.

1804—Twelfth Amendment to the Constitution rules that president and vice-president be elected separately. Alexander Hamilton is killed by Vice-President Aaron Burr in a duel. Orleans Territory is established. Napoleon crowns himself emperor of France. Franklin Pierce is born in Hillsborough Lower Village, New Hampshire.

1805—Thomas Jefferson begins his second term as president. Lewis and Clark expedition reaches the Pacific Ocean.

1806—Coinage of silver dollars is stopped; resumes in 1836.

1807—Aaron Burr is acquitted in treason trial. Embargo Act closes U.S. ports to trade.

1808—James Madison is elected president. Congress outlaws importing slaves from Africa. Andrew Johnson is born in Raleigh, North Carolina.

1809—Abraham Lincoln is born near Hodgenville, Kentucky.

1810—U.S. population is 7,240,000.

1811—William Henry Harrison defeats Indians at Tippecanoe. Monroe is named secretary of state.

1812—Louisiana becomes a state. U.S. declares war on Britain (War of 1812). James Madison is reelected president. Napoleon invades Russia.

1813—British forces take Fort Niagara and Buffalo, New York.

1814—Francis Scott Key writes "The Star-Spangled Banner." British troops burn much of Washington, D.C., including the White House. Treaty of Ghent ends War of 1812. James Monroe becomes secretary of war.

1815—Napoleon meets his final defeat at Battle of Waterloo.

1816—James Monroe is elected president. Indiana becomes a state.

1817—Mississippi becomes a state. Construction on Erie Canal begins.

1818—Illinois enters the Union. The present thirteen-stripe flag is adopted. Border between U.S. and Canada is agreed upon.

1819—Alabama becomes a state. U.S. purchases Florida from Spain. Thomas Jefferson establishes the University of Virginia.

1820—James Monroe is reelected. In the Missouri Compromise, Maine enters the Union as a free (non-slave) state.

1821—Missouri enters the Union as a slave state. Santa Fe Trail opens the American Southwest. Mexico declares independence from Spain. Napoleon Bonaparte dies.

1822—U.S. recognizes Mexico and Colombia. Liberia in Africa is founded as a home for freed slaves. Ulysses S. Grant is born in Point Pleasant, Ohio. Rutherford B. Hayes is born in Delaware, Ohio.

1823—Monroe Doctrine closes North and South America to European colonizing or invasion.

1824—House of Representatives elects John Quincy Adams president when none of the four candidates wins a majority in national election. Mexico becomes a republic.

1825—Erie Canal is opened. U.S. population is 11,300,000.

1826—Thomas Jefferson and John Adams both die on July 4, the fiftieth anniversary of the Declaration of Independence.

1828—Andrew Jackson is elected president. Tariff of Abominations is passed, cutting imports.

1829—James Madison attends Virginia's constitutional convention. Slavery is abolished in Mexico. Chester A. Arthur is born in Fairfield, Vermont.

1830—Indian Removal Act to resettle Indians west of the Mississippi is approved.

1831—James Monroe dies in New York City. James A. Garfield is born in Orange, Ohio. Cyrus McCormick develops his reaper.

1832—Andrew Jackson, nominated by the new Democratic Party, is reelected president.

1833—Britain abolishes slavery in its colonies. Benjamin Harrison is born in North Bend, Ohio.

1835—Federal government becomes debt-free for the first time.

1836—Martin Van Buren becomes president. Texas wins independence from Mexico. Arkansas joins the Union. James Madison dies at Montpelier, Virginia.

1837—Michigan enters the Union. U.S. population is 15,900,000. Grover Cleveland is born in Caldwell, New Jersey.

1840—William Henry Harrison is elected president.

1841—President Harrison dies in Washington, D.C., one month after inauguration. Vice-President John Tyler succeeds him.

1843—William McKinley is born in Niles, Ohio.

1844—James Knox Polk is elected president. Samuel Morse sends first telegraphic message.

1845—Texas and Florida become states. Potato famine in Ireland causes massive emigration from Ireland to U.S. Andrew Jackson dies near Nashville, Tennessee.

1846—Iowa enters the Union. War with Mexico begins.

1847—U.S. captures Mexico City.

1848—Zachary Taylor becomes president. Treaty of Guadalupe Hidalgo ends Mexico-U.S. war. Wisconsin becomes a state.

1849—James Polk dies in Nashville, Tennessee.

1850—President Taylor dies in Washington, D.C.; Vice-President Millard Fillmore succeeds him. California enters the Union, breaking tie between slave and free states.

1852—Franklin Pierce is elected president.

1853—Gadsen Purchase transfers Mexican territory to U.S.

1854—"War for Bleeding Kansas" is fought between slave and free states.

1855—Czar Nicholas I of Russia dies, succeeded by Alexander II.

1856—James Buchanan is elected president. In Massacre of Potawatomi Creek, Kansas-slavers are murdered by free-staters. Woodrow Wilson is born in Staunton, Pennsylvania.

1857—William Howard Taft is born in Cincinnati, Ohio.

1858—Minnesota enters the Union. Theodore Roosevelt is born in New York City.

1859—Oregon becomes a state.

1860—Abraham Lincoln is elected president; South Carolina secedes from the Union in protest.

1861—Arkansas, Tennessee, North Carolina, and Virginia secede. Kansas enters the Union as a free state. Civil War begins.

1862—Union forces capture Fort Henry, Roanoke Island, Fort Donelson, Jacksonville, and New Orleans; Union armies are defeated at the battles of Bull Run and Fredericksburg. Martin Van Buren dies in Kinderhook, New York. John Tyler dies near Charles City, Virginia.

1863—Lincoln issues Emancipation Proclamation: all slaves held in rebelling territories are declared free. West Virginia becomes a state.

1864—Abraham Lincoln is reelected. Nevada becomes a state.

1865—Lincoln is assassinated in Washington, D.C., and succeeded by Andrew Johnson. U.S. Civil War ends on May 26. Thirteenth Amendment abolishes slavery. Warren G. Harding is born in Blooming Grove, Ohio.

1867—Nebraska becomes a state. U.S. buys Alaska from Russia for $7,200,000. Reconstruction Acts are passed.

1868—President Johnson is impeached for violating Tenure of Office Act, but is acquitted by Senate. Ulysses S. Grant is elected president. Fourteenth Amendment prohibits voting discrimination. James Buchanan dies in Lancaster, Pennsylvania.

1869—Franklin Pierce dies in Concord, New Hampshire.

1870—Fifteenth Amendment gives blacks the right to vote.

1872—Grant is reelected over Horace Greeley. General Amnesty Act pardons ex-Confederates. Calvin Coolidge is born in Plymouth Notch, Vermont.

1874—Millard Fillmore dies in Buffalo, New York. Herbert Hoover is born in West Branch, Iowa.

1875—Andrew Johnson dies in Carter's Station, Tennessee.

1876—Colorado enters the Union. "Custer's last stand": he and his men are massacred by Sioux Indians at Little Big Horn, Montana.

1877—Rutherford B. Hayes is elected president as all disputed votes are awarded to him.

1880—James A. Garfield is elected president.

1881—President Garfield is assassinated and dies in Elberon, New Jersey. Vice-President Chester A. Arthur succeeds him.

1882—U.S. bans Chinese immigration. Franklin D. Roosevelt is born in Hyde Park, New York.

1884—Grover Cleveland is elected president.

1885—Ulysses S. Grant dies in Mount McGregor, New York.

1886—Statue of Liberty is dedicated. Chester A. Arthur dies in New York City.

1888—Benjamin Harrison is elected president.

1889—North Dakota, South Dakota, Washington, and Montana become states.

1890—Dwight D. Eisenhower is born in Denison, Texas. Idaho and Wyoming become states.

1892—Grover Cleveland is elected president.

1893—Rutherford B. Hayes dies in Fremont, Ohio.

1896—William McKinley is elected president. Utah becomes a state.

1898—U.S. declares war on Spain over Cuba.

1900—McKinley is reelected. Boxer Rebellion against foreigners in China begins.

1901—McKinley is assassinated by anarchist Leon Czolgosz in Buffalo, New York; Theodore Roosevelt becomes president. Benjamin Harrison dies in Indianapolis, Indiana.

1902—U.S. acquires perpetual control over Panama Canal.

1903—Alaskan frontier is settled.

1904—Russian-Japanese War breaks out. Theodore Roosevelt wins presidential election.

1905—Treaty of Portsmouth signed, ending Russian-Japanese War.

1906—U.S. troops occupy Cuba.

1907—President Roosevelt bars all Japanese immigration. Oklahoma enters the Union.

1908—William Howard Taft becomes president. Grover Cleveland dies in Princeton, New Jersey. Lyndon B. Johnson is born near Stonewall, Texas.

1909—NAACP is founded under W.E.B. DuBois

1910—China abolishes slavery.

1911—Chinese Revolution begins. Ronald Reagan is born in Tampico, Illinois.

1912—Woodrow Wilson is elected president. Arizona and New Mexico become states.

1913—Federal income tax is introduced in U.S. through the Sixteenth Amendment. Richard Nixon is born in Yorba Linda, California. Gerald Ford is born in Omaha, Nebraska.

1914—World War I begins.

1915—British liner *Lusitania* is sunk by German submarine.

1916—Wilson is reelected president.

1917—U.S. breaks diplomatic relations with Germany. Czar Nicholas of Russia abdicates as revolution begins. U.S. declares war on Austria-Hungary. John F. Kennedy is born in Brookline, Massachusetts.

1918—Wilson proclaims "Fourteen Points" as war aims. On November 11, armistice is signed between Allies and Germany.

1919—Eighteenth Amendment prohibits sale and manufacture of intoxicating liquors. Wilson presides over first League of Nations; wins Nobel Peace Prize. Theodore Roosevelt dies in Oyster Bay, New York.

1920—Nineteenth Amendment (women's suffrage) is passed. Warren Harding is elected president.

1921—Adolf Hitler's stormtroopers begin to terrorize political opponents.

1922—Irish Free State is established. Soviet states form USSR. Benito Mussolini forms Fascist government in Italy.

1923—President Harding dies in San Francisco, California; he is succeeded by Vice-President Calvin Coolidge.

1924—Coolidge is elected president. Woodrow Wilson dies in Washington, D.C. James Carter is born in Plains, Georgia. George Bush is born in Milton, Massachusetts.

1925—Hitler reorganizes Nazi Party and publishes first volume of *Mein Kampf*.

1926—Fascist youth organizations founded in Germany and Italy. Republic of Lebanon proclaimed.

1927—Stalin becomes Soviet dictator. Economic conference in Geneva attended by fifty-two nations.

1928—Herbert Hoover is elected president. U.S. and many other nations sign Kellogg-Briand pacts to outlaw war.

1929—Stock prices in New York crash on "Black Thursday"; the Great Depression begins.

1930—Bank of U.S. and its many branches close (most significant bank failure of the year). William Howard Taft dies in Washington, D.C.

1931—Emigration from U.S. exceeds immigration for first time as Depression deepens.

1932—Franklin D. Roosevelt wins presidential election in a Democratic landslide.

1933—First concentration camps are erected in Germany. U.S. recognizes USSR and resumes trade. Twenty-First Amendment repeals prohibition. Calvin Coolidge dies in Northampton, Massachusetts.

1934—Severe dust storms hit Plains states. President Roosevelt passes U.S. Social Security Act.

1936—Roosevelt is reelected. Spanish Civil War begins. Hitler and Mussolini form Rome-Berlin Axis.

1937—Roosevelt signs Neutrality Act.

1938—Roosevelt sends appeal to Hitler and Mussolini to settle European problems amicably.

1939—Germany takes over Czechoslovakia and invades Poland, starting World War II.

1940—Roosevelt is reelected for a third term.

1941—Japan bombs Pearl Harbor, U.S. declares war on Japan. Germany and Italy declare war on U.S.; U.S. then declares war on them.

1942—Allies agree not to make separate peace treaties with the enemies. U.S. government transfers more than 100,000 Nisei (Japanese-Americans) from west coast to inland concentration camps.

1943—Allied bombings of Germany begin.

1944—Roosevelt is reelected for a fourth term. Allied forces invade Normandy on D-Day.

1945—President Franklin D. Roosevelt dies in Warm Springs, Georgia; Vice-President Harry S. Truman succeeds him. Mussolini is killed; Hitler commits suicide. Germany surrenders. U.S. drops atomic bomb on Hiroshima; Japan surrenders: end of World War II.

1946—U.N. General Assembly holds its first session in London. Peace conference of twenty-one nations is held in Paris.

1947—Peace treaties are signed in Paris. "Cold War" is in full swing.

1948—U.S. passes Marshall Plan Act, providing $17 billion in aid for Europe. U.S. recognizes new nation of Israel. India and Pakistan become free of British rule. Truman is elected president.

1949—Republic of Eire is proclaimed in Dublin. Russia blocks land route access from Western Germany to Berlin; airlift begins. U.S., France, and Britain agree to merge their zones of occupation in West Germany. Apartheid program begins in South Africa.

1950—Riots in Johannesburg, South Africa, against apartheid. North Korea invades South Korea. U.N. forces land in South Korea and recapture Seoul.

1951—Twenty-Second Amendment limits president to two terms.

1952—Dwight D. Eisenhower resigns as supreme commander in Europe and is elected president.

1953—Stalin dies; struggle for power in Russia follows. Rosenbergs are executed for espionage.

1954—U.S. and Japan sign mutual defense agreement.

1955—Blacks in Montgomery, Alabama, boycott segregated bus lines.

1956—Eisenhower is reelected president. Soviet troops march into Hungary.

1957—U.S. agrees to withdraw ground forces from Japan. Russia launches first satellite, *Sputnik*.

1958—European Common Market comes into being. Alaska becomes the forty-ninth state. Fidel Castro begins war against Batista government in Cuba.

1959—Hawaii becomes fiftieth state. Castro becomes premier of Cuba. De Gaulle is proclaimed president of the Fifth Republic of France.

1960—Historic debates between Senator John F. Kennedy and Vice-President Richard Nixon are televised. Kennedy is elected president. Brezhnev becomes president of USSR.

1961—Berlin Wall is constructed. Kennedy and Khrushchev confer in Vienna. In Bay of Pigs incident, Cubans trained by CIA attempt to overthrow Castro.

1962—U.S. military council is established in South Vietnam.

1963—Riots and beatings by police and whites mark civil rights demonstrations in Birmingham, Alabama; 30,000 troops are called out, Martin Luther King, Jr., is arrested. Freedom marchers descend on Washington, D.C., to demonstrate. President Kennedy is assassinated in Dallas, Texas; Vice-President Lyndon B. Johnson is sworn in as president.

1964—U.S. aircraft bomb North Vietnam. Johnson is elected president. Herbert Hoover dies in New York City.

1965—U.S. combat troops arrive in South Vietnam.

1966—Thousands protest U.S. policy in Vietnam. National Guard quells race riots in Chicago.

1967—Six-Day War between Israel and Arab nations.

1968—Martin Luther King, Jr., is assassinated in Memphis, Tennessee. Senator Robert Kennedy is assassinated in Los Angeles. Riots and police brutality take place at Democratic National Convention in Chicago. Richard Nixon is elected president. Czechoslovakia is invaded by Soviet troops.

1969—Dwight D. Eisenhower dies in Washington, D.C. Hundreds of thousands of people in several U.S. cities demonstrate against Vietnam War.

1970—Four Vietnam War protesters are killed by National Guardsmen at Kent State University in Ohio.

1971—Twenty-Sixth Amendment allows eighteen-year-olds to vote.

1972—Nixon visits Communist China; is reelected president in near-record landslide. Watergate affair begins when five men are arrested in the Watergate hotel complex in Washington, D.C. Nixon announces resignations of aides Haldeman, Ehrlichman, and Dean and Attorney General Kleindienst as a result of Watergate-related charges. Harry S. Truman dies in Kansas City, Missouri.

1973—Vice-President Spiro Agnew resigns; Gerald Ford is named vice-president. Vietnam peace treaty is formally approved after nineteen months of negotiations. Lyndon B. Johnson dies in San Antonio, Texas.

1974—As a result of Watergate cover-up, impeachment is considered; Nixon resigns and Ford becomes president. Ford pardons Nixon and grants limited amnesty to Vietnam War draft evaders and military deserters.

1975—U.S. civilians are evacuated from Saigon, South Vietnam, as Communist forces complete takeover of South Vietnam.

1976—U.S. celebrates its Bicentennial. James Earl Carter becomes president.

1977—Carter pardons most Vietnam draft evaders, numbering some 10,000.

1980—Ronald Reagan is elected president.

1981—President Reagan is shot in the chest in assassination attempt. Sandra Day O'Connor is appointed first woman justice of the Supreme Court.

1983—U.S. troops invade island of Grenada.

1984—Reagan is reelected president. Democratic candidate Walter Mondale's running mate, Geraldine Ferraro, is the first woman selected for vice-president by a major U.S. political party.

1985—Soviet Communist Party secretary Konstantin Chernenko dies; Mikhail Gorbachev succeeds him. U.S. and Soviet officials discuss arms control in Geneva. Reagan and Gorbachev hold summit conference in Geneva. Racial tensions accelerate in South Africa.

1986—Space shuttle *Challenger* explodes shortly after takeoff; crew of seven dies. U.S. bombs bases in Libya. Corazon Aquino defeats Ferdinand Marcos in Philippine presidential election.

1987—Iraqi missile rips the U.S. frigate *Stark* in the Persian Gulf, killing thirty-seven American sailors. Congress holds hearings to investigate sale of U.S. arms to Iran to finance Nicaraguan *contra* movement.

1988—George Bush is elected president. President Reagan and Soviet leader Gorbachev sign INF treaty, eliminating intermediate nuclear forces. Severe drought sweeps the United States.

Index

Page numbers in boldface type indicate illustrations.

About the Author

Zachary Kent grew up in Little Falls, New Jersey, and received an English degree from St. Lawrence University. Following college he worked at a New York City literary agency for two years and then launched his writing career. To support himself while writing, he has worked as a taxi driver, a shipping clerk, and a house painter. Mr. Kent has had a lifelong interest in American history. Studying the U.S. presidents was his childhood hobby. His collection of presidential items includes books, pictures, and games, as well as several autographed letters.